Inspiration and Reflections for the School Leader

Dr. Kristilynn Turney

Copyright © 2021 Dr. Kristilynn Turney

All rights reserved. No portion of this book may be reproduced, stored in a retrieval system, or transmitted in any form or by any means—electronic, mechanical, photocopy recording, scanning, or other—except for brief quotations without the prior written permission of the author..

Published by Write the Book Now, an imprint of Perfect Time SHP LLC
ISBN: 978-1-73610282-4

Inspiration and Reflections for the School Leader

Introduction

In July 2019, I decided to take a leap of faith by creating my own educational and diversity consulting company. As I reflected on my platform, I went back to my over 20 years in education: Six years as a classroom teacher and 14 years as an administrator. Of those reflections, my greatest connections to God were when I was an assistant principal and building principal, which accounted for eight years of my career. I could not help but think how those were my most difficult yet rewarding years in education. Spending time encouraging staff and students and having a direct impact on so many parts of the day-to-day educational process was bittersweet. I laughed and cried almost daily and sometimes those tears were tears of joy when I was acknowledged for a job well done or when I helped a student or teacher accomplish something that they never thought possible. Through it all, the greatest emotion was joy. Each day, I had a joyful and thankful spirit and I kept the faith that not only could I do the job and do it well, but I could have a tremendous impact.

During my final year as a building principal and two weeks before our accreditation audit, my mom passed away. I was heartbroken! I mean crushed to pieces. My mom was my very best friend! She helped me carry the load of being a building principal by watching my children for evening events, cooking and cleaning, and even helping them with homework. The days and months after her passing were some of the darkest days of my principalship. Yet, I managed as I had always managed and that was through God's grace, love, and healing.

This book is a powerful tool designed to encourage school leaders no matter what they are going through, to be prayerful, focused and reflective. Each scripture is matched with a brief poem, scenario, and prayer. Each scripture is a quick dose of faith and encouragement to get you through the day. At the end of each segment, you can reflect and connect so that you can have the motivation to keep going strong.

Psalm 121: "I will lift up mine eyes unto the hills from whence cometh my help. My help cometh from the Lord!"

Inspiration and Reflections for the School Leader

Dr. Kristilynn Turney and my beautiful mother, Joann Burnett

About the Author

Dr. Kristilynn Turney is a proud Cincinnatian. She graduated from North College Hill High School at the height of major community and demographic changes. She was a recipient of a track scholarship to Bowling Green State University (BGSU) in Bowling Green, Ohio where she ran varsity track for four years, became a member of Sigma Gamma Rho Sorority, Incorporated and served as the National Pan-Hellenic Council, Inc. (NPHC) President for two years. Kristilynn graduated from BGSU with a Bachelor's in Secondary Education Communications. After teaching for one year, Dr. Kristilynn Turney began her Master's Degree in which she majored in Educational Administration at Xavier University (XU). She went on to receive her Principal's and Superintendent's license from XU as well. After serving in administration for six years, Kristilynn began her doctoral journey at Capella University and finished three years later with anEducational Doctorate (Ed.D.) in Educational Management and Leadership.

Dr. Kristilynn Turney is the CEO and founder of Dr. Kristilynn Turney, LLC and EdPD Unlimited, LLC. She specializes in Educational Leadership and Diversity Consulting.

Dr. Kristilynn Turney has served in public education for 20 years in the Greater Cincinnati and Dayton areas. She began her career as an English, Theatre, and Public Speaking Teacher. She was also a School Improvement Consultant and Literacy Coach for Hamilton County Educational Service Center. She then served as an assistant principal at Winton Woods High School. In 2012, Dr. Turney became the first African-American Principal at Fairfield Middle School and in 2014, she became the first African-American Principal and only the third female Principal at Colerain High School. She ended her career in public education as a district level administrator where she was a curriculum director and human resources/diversity director. She maintains Ohio Education Licenses in: All Communications (7-12), Principal (5-12), and Superintendent (P-12).

Currently, Dr. Kristilynn Turney works with Public, Private, and Charter Schools in the areas of School Improvement, Diversity, and Leadership and Mentoring. She has also published numerous articles about topics that she is most passionate about such as: Teachers of Color, Leaders and Zero-Sum Thinking, and English Language Learners. Throughout Dr. Turney's work, she has successfully engaged thousands of people in the process and has solicited help and guidance from many stakeholders of diverse backgrounds. While this has not been an easy task, especially when oftentimes she did not know the stakeholders prior to beginning the work, she made it seamless through building quick relationships through engaging activities, tasks and social, and professional connections.

In her "free-time" Dr. Turney enjoys spending time with her husband, Larry, and four kids; Kamille, Carson, Lailah and Lennox. She spends many days and weekends chasing their many activities and sports. Kristilynn is also an active member of her community and church and enjoys traveling, reading, exercising, spending time with extended family and friends and online shopping. She credits her success to her mother, Joan Burnett, who passed away in 2016. Her mother taught her grace, perseverance, strength, and to believe in God through all things!

Dr. Kristilynn Turney

Acknowledgements

To my brother, Tony Robinson: Thank you for the support and inspiration to write this book. Thank you for pushing me through this journey and many others. You believe in me for me! May we write many more books together.

To my dad: Thank you for the love and support to keep going.

To my friends, the School Leaders: Every day you lead, manage, challenge, motivate, and inspire. May God continue to bless you and your work!

May this book inspire you and allow you to reflect on your purpose. Keep up the great work. We are all cheering and praying with and for you!

This book was written during the COVID-19 pandemic. I was working as an Independent Consultant and Professor in March 2020 when the news broke that schools would be shutting down indefinitely. Of course my first thoughts went to my own children being home with me and how I would juggle their full-time at home education and my work as well but then my next thoughts went to the school administrators. How will they manage their staff? What practices will they put in place to make sure that all students learn at home? How will they prepare to return back to school? For one of the first times I was glad that I was not in charge of a building or district and quite frankly I was afraid. All I could do was pray!

Positive (adjective): Consisting in or characterized by the presence or possession of features or qualities rather than their absence.

Reflection:

Reflect on a positive experience as an administrator. Who did this experience involve and how did it make you feel? What can you do to replicate this positive experience again?

_____

_____

_____

_____

_____

_____

_____

_____

Words of Inspiration:

"I've missed more than 9,000 shots in my career. I've lost almost 300 games. Twenty-six times I've been trusted to take the game winning shot and missed. I've failed over and over and over again in my life and that is why I succeed."

– Michael Jordan

Do not be conformed to this world, but be transformed by the renewal of your mind, that by testing you may discern what is the will of God, what is good and acceptable and perfect.

Romans 12: 2

My thoughts:

I am reminded of my days as principal of Fairfield Middle School. At the time it was the largest middle school in the state of Ohio with 1700 seventh and eighth graders. As a part of our PBS (Positive Behavior Support) System students earned tickets throughout the year. They could save them or redeem them for monthly quarterly rewards. One of the middle of the year rewards was throwing a pie in the principal's face at an assembly. Well one young man made it his special mission to save his tickets to be able to throw a pie in my face. He reminded me every chance he saw me, which was almost daily, that he was going to throw a pie in my face. When the big awards assembly came, this student took great pride in coming forth with his collected tickets to throw a pie in my face. He did and he got me good! He then wanted to take a picture with me so that he could show his family and friends his accomplishment. With a face covered in cream filling, I was happy that he was happy so I gave the camera a great big smile.

A few months later at the eighth grade celebration this student walked up to me with his hands behind his back. Knowing that this was not the time or the place for another pie smashing, I asked him what was behind his back. He grinned and I began to think, "Oh no, he's about to pie me again and this time I can discipline him for it." He pulled out a framed picture of us from that fateful day. I smiled and we both laughed and hugged.

While I may have never had a positive experience on this young man's academics, I did have a positive experience in his time in middle school. He worked hard to collect tickets so that he could "pie me" and it was truly a positive experience and honor to get "ped" by him.

Faith (noun): Complete trust and confidence in someone or something.

Reflection:

Think of a time as an administrator when all you had was faith that something was going to work. What did faith sound and look like?

_____

_____

_____

_____

_____

_____

_____

Words of Inspiration:

"Faith is the substance of things hoped for, the evidence of things not seen."

Hebrews 11:1.

For I know the thoughts that I think toward you, says the Lord, thoughts of peace and not of evil, to give you a future and a hope."

Jeremiah 29:11.

Faith is taking the first step even when you don't see the whole staircase.

— Martin Luther King Jr.

My thoughts:

Being a school administrator can be rewarding and challenging. In the good times we celebrate and reflect on God's grace and kindness. In the challenging times we remember the positive times with the vision and foresight to know that it can and will get better. I am reminded of a sermon in which at the beginning the pastor prayed "make my job easy." Her prayer was "Dear Lord. I cannot do this without you so as I go along my journey 'make my job easy.' It is in your mighty name that I pray. Amen!" What a short and simple prayer! It was so short and simple that I questioned its power. A week later when I was laboring over the master schedule, thinking about how I will balance 1700 kids, across 14 teams with varying themes and challenges of Orchestra only being offered in the morning, Band only offered in the afternoon, teacher certifications who can only teach certain grade levels, and testing accountability measures; I could only pray. So I tried it "Dear Lord. I cannot do this without you so as I make this master schedule 'make my job easy.' That was on a Friday. I left the stack of requests on my desk but I could not stay away for long. The next morning, a Saturday, I got up with a different energy and a fire to go into my office and try to work through the master schedule, yet again. As I looked at the daunting task I began to tackle it. For several minutes it looked like gibberish and I still found myself with 70 kids in one Honors English Class. Then it hit me. What if I do this? I moved a single teacher and it was almost like dominos falling. Within minutes, I had a solution that helped me to plug in the schedule and in four hours, by 1pm I was headed home. My simple prayer of "make my job easy" worked. For many years as administrator thereafter, I said that same prayer. It was almost like I was looking up at the mountain and saying "get out of my way, mountain!"

Negative (adjective): (of a person, attitude, or situation) not desirable or optimistic.

Reflection:

Sometimes teachers, students, and parents can forget our feelings and our dedication to education. Reflect on a time when a teacher, student, or parent put you in a negative mood or caused negative emotions.

_____

_____

_____

_____

_____

_____

_____

_____

Dr. Kristilynn Turney

Words of Inspiration:

An anxious heart weighs man down, but a kind word cheers him up.

Proverbs 12:25

If you accept the expectations of others, especially negative ones, then you never will change the outcome.

— Michael Jordan

My thoughts:

When I reflect on the negative experiences as an administrator, very few of these experiences come from students but in fact from their parents. I will spare you all of the negative encounters but instead will remind you that sometimes parents have negative experiences from their own educational pasts. These negative experiences are passed down and can be rubbed off onto their students and/or are taken out on current school figures. Although it may be difficult, negative experiences with parents or anyone for that matter, cannot be taken personally. I always like to think that behaviors are not always reflective of the one on one situation but may be a result of other underlying problems or concerns. Here's a quick word of advice: If as an administrator you know that what you have done has been in the best interest of students and according to the school's or district's policy, that may be the greatest peace you take away from a negative situation. Move on and know that it is not always your fault.

Tired (adjective): In need of sleep or rest; weary.

Reflection:

Being an educator can be tiring. Now multiply that by at least five times and that is how an administrator feels. What do you do to care for yourself? How do you unwind, destress, and rest? If you are not currently doing anything, what would you like to do or try in the next month.

_____

_____

_____

_____

_____

_____

Words of Inspiration:

"Come to Me, all you who labor and are heavy laden, and I will give you rest. Take My yoke upon you and learn from Me, for I am gentle and lowly in heart, and you will find rest for your souls. For My yoke is easy and My burden is light."

Matthew 11:28-30.

Do you not know? Have you not heard? The LORD is the everlasting God, the Creator of the ends of the earth. He will not grow tired or weary, and his understanding no one can fathom. He gives strength to the weary and increases the power of the weak. Even youths grow tired and weary, and young men stumble and fall; but those who hope in the LORD will renew their strength. They will soar on wings like eagles; they will run and not grow weary, they will walk and not be faint.

Isaiah 40: 28-31

Tired, tired with nothing, tired with everything, tired with the world's weight he had never chosen to bear.

— F. Scott Fitzgerald

My thoughts: :

In my second year as a high school principal, I wanted to take my family to Gatlinburg, TN around Christmas for a weekend trip. Due to various scheduling conflicts, the only time that we could go was the weekend before Christmas and that Friday was the last day before Winter Break. With the blessing from my administrative team, I missed school that Friday to take a quick getaway. The trip included my husband, four kids, and my mom. We went to Dolly's (Dixie Stampede) and enjoyed the sights and sounds of the season. I felt bad about leaving but I knew that my building was in good hands. I also knew that the time away was great for my physical and mental health. It wasn't until a month later to the day when my mom passed that I truly realized the value of that trip.

Sometimes as administrators we get so lost in doing for others that we forget to do for ourselves and our families. Thank God I took time out of my busy schedule to take that short, weekend trip. I will never forget it.

Stressed (adjective): Experiencing mental or emotional strain or tension.

Reflection:

How do you avoid stressful situations? What are some ways that you organize your work or structure your day to avoid excess stress?

_____

_____

_____

_____

_____

_____

_____

Words of Inspiration:

"Have I not commanded you? Be strong and of good courage; do not be afraid, nor be dismayed, for the Lord your God is with you wherever you go."

Joshua 1:9.

"Work hard for what you want because it won't come to you without a fight. You have to be strong and courageous and know that you can do anything you put your mind to. If somebody puts you down or criticizes you, just keep on believing in yourself and turn it into something positive."

– Leah LaBelle

My thoughts:

One thing that I do to avoid stressful situations is plan ahead. I also worked to balance my personal and professional life by alternating early work days with late work days. So for example, I made it a practice to arrive to work an hour early on Mondays and Wednesdays and stay an hour late on Tuesdays and Thursdays, Fridays were almost always by "shorter" work days. This process allowed me to avoid working longer hours at home in the evenings and helped me stay organized to meet the demands of work and home life.

Excited (adjective): Very enthusiastic and eager.

Reflection:

What makes you excited about your work? Describe your excitement and how you celebrate a job well done.

_____

_____

_____

_____

_____

_____

_____

_____

_____

_____

Words of Inspiration:

But those who trust in the Lord for help will find their strength renewed. They will rise on wings like eagles; they will run and not get weary; they will walk and not grow weak.

Isaiah 40: 31

I feel sorry for the person who can't get genuinely excited about his work. Not only will he never be satisfied, but he will never achieve anything worthwhile.

— Walter Chrysler

My thoughts:

I love sports! During my time as a principal, I was blessed to celebrate my student successes beyond the classroom and on the athletic fields as well. From state championship football games to buzzer beating regional basketball tournaments I was excited to be a part of the pride and publicity that such events brought to our school and community. It was times like these in the midst of state testing, changing mandates, and unbelievable deadlines that kept me motivated and excited about my work.

Motivated (verb): Provide someone with a motive for doing something.

Reflection:

What motivates you to continue being an administrator? Why?

_____

_____

_____

_____

_____

_____

_____

_____

_____

_____

Words of Inspiration:

What, then, shall we say in response to these things? If God is for us, who can be against us?

Romans 8:31

Irish Blessing

May the road rise up to meet you.
May the wind always be at your back.
May the sun shine warm upon your face,
and rains fall soft upon your fields.
And until we meet again,
May God hold you in the palm of His hand.

My thoughts:

I have always enjoyed working with students and teaching others. My passion for teaching began in my backyard in the heat of the summer where I would teach my cousins and neighborhood kids how to read and write. While I attempted to dodge the profession of teaching once in college, even toying with the idea of becoming a journalist, I knew where my heart was. I knew deep down inside that no matter what happened the previous day in my classroom or the school, I would be motivated to get up and do it all again the next day. The students depended on me and I could not let them down. I even hated being sick and missing school because I knew that a lost day of my instruction could be detrimental to some of my students.

Frustrated (adjective): Feeling or expressing distress and annoyance, especially because of inability to change or achieve something.

Reflection:

Think of the time when you became so frustrated that you acted out of character. What triggered your response? If you could do it all over again, how would you respond differently?

_____

_____

_____

_____

_____

_____

_____

_____

Words of Inspiration:

"Be anxious for nothing, but in everything by prayer and supplication, with thanksgiving, let your requests be made known to God; and the peace of God, which surpasses all understanding, will guard your hearts and minds through Christ Jesus. Finally, brethren, whatever things are true, whatever things are noble, whatever things are just, whatever things are pure, whatever things are lovely, whatever things are of good report, if there is any virtue and if there is anything praiseworthy—meditate on these things."

Philippians 4:6-8.

Forget perfect on the first try. In the face of frustration, your best tool is a few deep breaths, and remembering that you can do anything once you've practiced two hundred times. Seriously.

— Andrea Buchanan

My thoughts:

If I have experienced it once, I have experienced it a million times as an administrator and that is changing targets and changing expectations. This leads to frustration, anger, and an attitude of defeat. Due to standards, shifting trends, and focus points education can be one of the hardest professions. But I am reminded of the scripture from John 16:33: "I have told you these things, so that in me you may have peace. In this world you will have trouble. But take heart! I have overcome the world." This scripture gives me peace and reminds me to seek strength from the Lord.

Lost (adjective): Unable to find one's way; not knowing one's whereabouts.

Reflection:

What are some things you have "lost" as a result of being an administrator? How can you regain these "lost" things back?

_____

_____

_____

_____

_____

_____

_____

Words of Inspiration:

Sometimes God's blessings are not in what He gives; but in what He takes away.

For nothing is hidden that will not be made manifest, nor is anything secret that will not be known and come to light.

Luke 8:17

So have no fear of them, for nothing is covered that will not be revealed, or hidden that will not be known.

Matthew 10:26

Sometimes being lost is the best way to find yourself.

— LJ Vanier

My thoughts:

As an administrator, I felt that I lost time with loved ones, structure and a piece of my sanity. Thank God for restoration because whether it was through a well needed holiday or summer break, or even a surprise snow day; I was able to be restored, reenergized, and motivated to continue going. Make a vow to yourself to keep some sacred time for finding your way back. This can be a weekend afternoon, break times, or designated evening. Take time for you!

Confused (adjective): (of a person) unable to think clearly; bewildered.

Reflection:

As an administrator what has caused confusion or bewilderment? How did you respond to that challenge?

_____

_____

_____

_____

_____

_____

_____

_____

Words of Inspiration:

For God is not a God of confusion but of peace. As in all the churches of the saints.

Corinthians 14: 33

Think over what I say, for the Lord will give you understanding in everything.

Timothy 2:7

Life is similar to a bus ride.

The journey begins when we board the bus.

We meet people along our way of which some are strangers, some friends and some strangers yet to be friends.

There are stops at intervals and people board in.

At times some of these people make their presence felt, leaving an impact through their grace and beauty on us fellow passengers while on other occasions they remain indifferent.

But then it is important for some people to make an exit, to get down and walk the paths they were destined to because if people always made an entrance and never left either for the better or worse, then we would feel suffocated and confused like those people in the bus, the purpose of the journey would lose its essence and the journey altogether would neither be worthwhile nor smooth.

— Chirag Tulsiani

My thoughts:

As a school leader, you are not allowed to be confused, misspeak, question, doubt, or fear. Sounds pretty unreasonable, right? Of course it does but sometimes that is the perception. Give yourself some grace. Allow yourself to make mistakes; don't beat yourself over confusion yet pray for clarity and peace.

Determined (adjective): Having made a firm decision and being resolved not to change it.

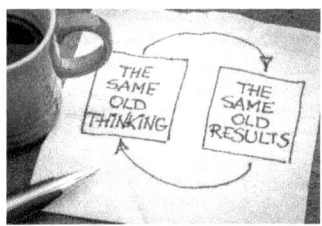

Reflection:

Think about a time when you had to hold a firm yet unpopular decision. How did you handle it?

_____

_____

_____

_____

_____

_____

_____

_____

_____

Words of Inspiration:

Be strong and courageous. Do not fear or be in dread of them, for it is the Lord your God who goes with you. He will not leave you or forsake you.

Deuteronomy 31: 6

"Fight for the things that you care about, but do it in a way that will lead others to join you."-

— Ruth Bader Ginsberg

My thoughts:

Decision making can be tough. When making decisions, be careful to consider all sides, factors, and outcomes. One thing that I used to do as a principal was play out my decisions based on how each stakeholder would respond. I would think to myself, if I do something one way what will the parents, students, and fellow administrators say or think. This simple process allowed me to make the best decisions and consider all elements before making and sharing the decision.

Focused (verb): (of a person or their eyes) adapt to the prevailing level of light and become able to see clearly.

Reflection:

What project/activity are you focusing on right now? What is your plan to make it successful?

_____

_____

_____

_____

_____

_____

_____

Words of Inspiration:

And we know that in all things God works for the good of those who love him, who have been called according to his purpose.

Romans 8:28

Therefore we do not lose heart. Though outwardly we are wasting away, yet inwardly we are being renewed day by day. For our light and momentary troubles are achieving for us an eternal glory that far outweighs them all. So we fix our eyes not on what is seen, but on what is unseen, since what is seen is temporary, but what is unseen is eternal.

2 Corinthians 4: 16-18

Most people have no idea of the giant capacity we can immediately command when we focus all of our resources on mastering a single area of our lives.

— Anthony Robbins

My thoughts:

For me, it's easy to lose focus; I blame it on my undiagnosed ADHD. That's why as a school leader it is important to keep organizational tools including "Things to Do Lists" and calendars. Beyond these tools though, I always kept sight of our district and school goals by keeping a handwritten note card of important reminders. I would even highlight the current/quarterly goals. This allowed me to remain focused. Whenever I lost sight of my purpose and battled with my role as an administrator, I would refer back to that handwritten note card. For example, one year my school's goals were around the areas of Rigor, Relationships, and Relevance. Quite frequently, I found myself referring back to that card and thinking about how I encouraged and evaluated teachers based on rigorous and relevant classroom strategies and lessons and how I worked to build positive and sustainable relationships with students. Whatever you do, don't lose focus of your purpose!

Grit (verb): Continued effort to do or achieve something despite difficulties, failure, or opposition. The action or condition or an instance of persevering. STEADFASTNESS!

Reflection:

What has been something that you have remained steadfast about? What are some ways that you remained focused on that item?

_____

_____

_____

_____

_____

_____

Words of Inspiration:

"Let my teaching fall like rain and my words descend like dew, like showers on new grass, like abundant rain on tender plants."

Deuteronomy 32:2

"It's not the load that breaks you down, it's the way you carry it."

– Lou Holtz

My thoughts:

Sometimes what we do has very little to do with being smart, eloquent, or well studied. Our work can come down to sheer grit and our willingness to persevere through challenges and adversity. A common challenge are scores and the school's academic performance. Having served in School Improvement as an outside consultant, I always felt that the schools did not lack "good kids" or a "willing staff," yet they lacked sheer grit and perseverance to see their plans through. Time and time again, I would see schools adopt an idea and when it didn't work after a few weeks, months, or even after one single school year; they were ready to move to the next "Flavor of the Month." They never put in the work to make it work; especially because very few things happen overnight. It takes grit and steadfastness.

Commitment (noun): The resolve of teaching professionals to contribute honorable service to the classroom, to perform their duties with discipline and to standards, and to strive to successfully and ethically accomplish the mission despite adversity, obstacles, and challenge.

Reflection:

Think of something that you are committed to this school year. How is this different from previous years? How will you remain committed to this idea?

_____

_____

_____

_____

_____

Words of Inspiration:

"Fix these words of mine in your hearts and minds; tie them as symbols on your hands and bind them on your foreheads. Teach them to your children, talking about them when you sit at home and when you walk along the road, when you lie down and when you get up."

Deuteronomy 11:18-19

"Things may come to those who wait, but only the things left by those who hustle."

— Abraham Lincoln

My thoughts:

Being a school leader is truly a work of "heart." Very few of us do it for the money or fame. Instead, we do it for the love of the students, the passion for leading others, and the desire to promote positive change. When the days are long and the nights are short and sleepless; never forget your commitment to your role as a school leader.

Pride (noun): A feeling or deep pleasure or satisfaction derived from one's own achievements, the achievements of those with whom one is closely associated, or from qualities or possessions that are widely admired.

Reflection:

What does your school or district value the most? How do you uphold and support that pride?

___

___

___

___

___

___

Words of Inspiration:

For gaining wisdom and instruction; for understanding words of insight; for receiving instruction in prudent behavior, doing what is right and just and fair; for giving prudence to those who are simple, knowledge and discretion to the young

Proverbs 1:2-4

"We are what we repeatedly do. Excellence, then, is not an act, but a habit."

— Aristotle

My thoughts:

Each school has a sense of pride and what makes them unique. One school where I was the principal, I often joked to peers that it was "football, show choir, then God!" While that truly wasn't the case in my life, the culture lent itself to that sense of pride. I always put God first but I knew where the community stood. I felt that if I upheld my relationship with God as the school leader, I could support the things that the school community were most passionate about. They didn't have to know that I prayed through those halls every day and I'm certain that they did not know that I prayed for big football wins, show choir victories, and of course the safety and well-being of my school, the staff, and students.

Truth (noun): The property of being in accord with fact or reality. In everyday language, truth is typically ascribed to things that aim to represent reality or otherwise correspond to it, such as beliefs, propositions, and declarative sentences. Truth is usually held to be the opposite of falsity.

Reflection:

How do you fact-find and seek truth in your school or district? What methods and resources do you use?

_____

_____

_____

_____

_____

_____

_____

Words of Inspiration:

"Do your best to present yourself to God as one approved, a worker who does not need to be ashamed and who correctly handles the word of truth."

2 Timothy 2:15

An error does not become truth by reason of multiplied propagation, nor does truth become error because nobody sees it.

— Mahatma Gandhi

My thoughts:

One thing that I committed myself to as a school leader was truth. This was never difficult for me as I saw other leaders suffer from their consequences of being dishonest. I feared that demise and I always felt that no matter where I ended up, I wanted my good name to stand and go before me. Whether it's being loyal to a poor superior or "fudging the numbers," always let truth lead you. When all is said and done that may be all you have left and if that's the case then I am a witness, YOU WILL BE ALRIGHT!

Dedication (noun): A feeling of very strong support for or loyalty to someone or something.

Reflection:

Reflect on your most loyal staff or team members. What makes them so loyal? Is their loyalty based on you personally or is it loyalty to the position that you hold?

_____

_____

_____

_____

_____

_____

_____

Words of Inspiration:

"Therefore, my dear brothers and sisters, stand firm. Let nothing move you. Always give yourselves fully to the work of the Lord, because you know that your labor in the Lord is not in vain."

1 Corinthians 15:58

"Don't say you don't have enough time. You have exactly the same number of hours per day that were given to Helen Keller, Pasteur, Michelangelo, Mother Teresa, Leonardo da Vinci, Thomas Jefferson, and Albert Einstein."

— H. Jackson Brown Jr.

My thoughts:

Each morning before school I would ask God to bless my work so that others would see my good work and dedication and glorify God in Heaven! It was my daily mission to please God and I did that through my dedication to Him and my God-given role as a school leader.

Preparation (noun): The action or process of making something ready for use or service or of getting ready for some occasion, test, or duty

Reflection:

How do you prepare for a challenging day/week such as testing week, spirit week, or the week before a long break? What do you do?

_____

_____

_____

_____

_____

_____

_____

_____

Words of Inspiration:

"But in your hearts revere Christ as Lord. Always be prepared to give an answer to everyone who asks you to give the reason for the hope that you have. But do this with gentleness and respect."

1 Peter 3:15

There is no shortcut to achievement. Life requires thorough preparation - veneer isn't worth anything.

— George Washington Carver

My thoughts:

Sometimes as a principal, my head would spin in 1000 different directions. As soon as I put out one fire, here came a bigger one. As soon as I got "caught up" a new mountain of work would appear. That did not stop me from asking God to "prepare me for whatever was coming next." It reminded me of a song that we use to sing in church, "Prepare Ye The Way of the Lord." While the song was about making room for God's gifts, I would often hum it with the request that God would prepare to be mighty and strong in the next storm as a principal.

Passion (noun): Passion is a feeling of intense enthusiasm towards or compelling desire for someone or something. Passion can range from eager interest in or admiration for an idea, proposal, or cause; to enthusiastic enjoyment of an interest or activity; to strong attraction, excitement, or emotion towards a person.

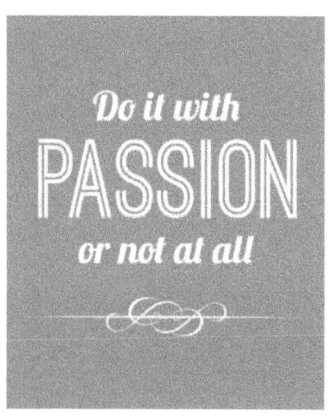

Reflection:

What about your role are you most passionate about? Why?

___

___

___

___

___

___

Words of Inspiration:

"So Christ himself gave the apostles, the prophets, the evangelists, the pastors and teachers, to equip his people for works of service, so that the body of Christ may be built up until we all reach unity in the faith and in the knowledge of the Son of God and become mature, attaining to the whole measure of the fullness of Christ. Then we will no longer be infants, tossed back and forth by the waves, and blown here and there by every wind of teaching and by the cunning and craftiness of people in their deceitful scheming. Instead, speaking the truth in love, we will grow to become in every respect the mature body of him who is the head, that is, Christ. From him the whole body, joined and held together by every supporting ligament, grows and builds itself up in love, as each part does its work."

Ephesians 4: 11-16

A passion for one's work makes life happier and work no longer work.

— Catherine Pulsifer

My thoughts:

I am a people person so I was always passionate about my students and staff. I made it my duty to always speak to everyone and make them feel special about being a part of our great school. A gentle smile, kind word, and enthusiastic spirit goes a long way in building a strong culture and climate.

Perseverance (noun): Steady persistence in a course of action, a purpose, a state, etc., especially in spite of difficulties, obstacles, or discouragement.

Reflection:

Think about a challenge or concern that you persevered through. What did you do to keep going and remain focused?

_____

_____

_____

_____

_____

_____

_____

_____

_____

Words of Inspiration:

Blessed is the man who remains steadfast under trial, for when he has stood the test he will receive the crown of life, which God has promised to those who love him.

James 1: 12

And let us not grow weary of doing good, for in due season we will reap, if we do not give up.

Galatians 6:9

Many of life's failures are people who did not realize how close they were to success when they gave up.

— Thomas Edison

"Young and old alike, teacher as well as student, cast lots for their duties."

1 Chronicles 25:8

My thoughts:

My passion for learning, teaching, and making a difference always kept me going. As I reflect on my time as a school administrator, I don't believe I "worked" much. I loved what I did so much I never felt like I was working. Even on the late nights and early mornings; I persevered out of love!

Justice (noun): The quality of being just; righteousness, equitableness, or moral rightness.

Reflection:

What does justice and fairness mean to you? How important is it to have a discipline policy that is fair for all students?

_____

_____

_____

_____

_____

_____

_____

_____

Words of Inspiration:

"The student is not above the teacher, nor a servant above his master."

Matthew 10:24

It is certain, in any case, that ignorance allied with power is the most ferocious enemy justice can have.

— James Baldwin

My thoughts:

The Lord is just and righteous and He wants us to be the same. You can never go wrong with doing the right thing. It may hurt at the time and you may even question if doing the wrong thing would please more people but in the end just do the right thing. That's what we teach our students, right? Why not live by your own words and expectations first!

Grace (noun):Unmerited divine assistance given to humans for their regeneration or sanctification

Reflection:

When have you offered grace to a student or teacher? Why did you decide to choose grace versus another option?

___

___

___

___

___

___

___

___

___

Words of Inspiration:

"We have different gifts, according to the grace given to each of us. If your gift is prophesying, then prophesy in accordance with your faith; if it is serving, then serve; if it is teaching, then teach;"

Romans 12:6-7

For grace is given not because we have done good works, but in order that we may be able to do them.

— Saint Augustine

My thoughts:

Sometimes I laugh to myself about how many students I "saved" and gave them a chance. How many discipline referrals did I combine and played "Let's make a deal!" I never thought I would be that type of administrator but I quickly learned that every student and their circumstance was different. Some students simply needed a little bit of grace.

I reflect on one student in particular who seemed to be living someplace else besides home. It was his Senior year and he had one goal and that was to graduate. Our school's policy was that students were to be in uniform-specific colors of collared shirts with 2-3 buttons and khaki or navy non-cargo pants. We always kept extra uniforms for emergency situations/accidents but not really for daily use. What started as the student asking me to borrow a uniform shirt one day turned into a nearly every day affair for the last few weeks of school. I never asked him his situation, I felt that I didn't need to know and I trusted that his need was genuine. "Mrs. Turney, may I borrow a uniform shirt." He would return it at the end of each school day and we washed extra uniforms a few times a week. I was just glad that he was in school and finishing his Senior year. What if I did not extend grace to that student? What if I questioned that student and made him feel uncomfortable? I can only assume that my actions "saved" him.

Endurance (noun): The ability to withstand hardship or adversity.

Reflection:

Administrators are no stranger to adversity. What gives you endurance to sustain such adversity?

_____

_____

_____

_____

_____

_____

_____

_____

_____

Words of Inspiration:

"For everything that was written in the past was written to teach us, so that through the endurance taught in the Scriptures and the encouragement they provide we might have hope."

Romans 15:4

No pain that we suffer, no trial that we experience is wasted. It ministers to our education, to the development of such qualities as patience, faith, fortitude and humility. All that we suffer and all that we endure, especially when we endure it patiently, builds up our characters, purifies our hearts, expands our souls, and makes us more tender and charitable, more worthy to be called the children of God . . . and it is through sorrow and suffering, toil and tribulation, that we gain the education that we come here to acquire and which will make us more like our Father and Mother in heaven.

— Orson F. Whitney

My thoughts:

Adversity does not have to mean someone is against you or plotting your downfall. Adversity as an administrator could mean a health problem for you or a loved one or another personal challenge that distracts you from your job. Time is filled with swift transitions. One day you're up, the next day you're down. But we know that God remains the same and that's why we must hold on to His unchanging hand. Through the good and the bad, God is still in control and we must trust that He will never leave nor forsake us.

Opportunity (noun): An appropriate or favorable time or occasion.

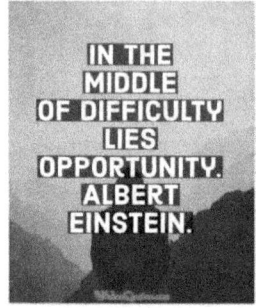

Reflection:

When in your career did you quickly and/or blindly jump at an opportunity? How did it make you feel? Was the outcome what you desired?

_____

_____

_____

_____

_____

_____

_____

_____

Words of Inspiration:

But he said to me, "My grace is sufficient for you, for my power is made perfect in weakness." Therefore I will boast all the more gladly of my weaknesses, so that the power of Christ may rest upon me. For the sake of Christ, then, I am content with weaknesses, insults, hardships, persecutions, and calamities. For when I am weak, then I am strong.

2 Corinthians 12: 9-10

To succeed, jump as quickly at opportunities as you do at conclusions.

— Benjamin Franklin

My thoughts:

Throughout my career, I waited on the Lord to lead me to the best opportunity. One year, I had 3 offerings for an assistant principal position. After careful evaluations, prayer, consideration and family consultation; God led me to the best job I ever had. I grew personally, professionally, spiritually, and I made a lot of lasting friendships. So my advice: "Wait on the Lord and be of good courage!"

Communication (noun): Communication is the act of conveying meanings from one entity or group to another through the use of mutually understood signs, symbols, and semiotic rules. The main steps inherent to all communication are: The formation of communicative motivation or reason. Message composition.

Reflection:

What are some of your communication norms? These can include how you communicate with your administrative team, staff, and/or parents.

_____

_____

_____

_____

_____

_____

_____

Words of Inspiration:

Know this, my beloved brothers: let every person be quick to hear, slow to speak, slow to anger

James 1:19

Then the Lord put out his hand and touched my mouth. And the Lord said to me, "Behold, I have put my words in your mouth.

Jeremiah 1: 9

Good communication is just as stimulating as black coffee, and just as hard to sleep after.

— Anne Morrow Lindbergh

My thoughts:

Once I became a principal, I reflected on previous experiences and what I would like to see done differently or better. In my previous years as an Assistant Principal, School Improvement Coach, and Teacher, I remember desiring more communication and being "in the know." I also wanted more opportunities to celebrate and acknowledge the great work of myself and peers. My reflections led me to creating a weekly newsletter. In the newsletter, I would share upcoming events, literacy tips/strategies, strategies for success for students from diverse backgrounds, and I would also feature a team or teacher of the week along with some pictures from their classroom. Not only was this a way to keep my team informed, it was also a way to promote building goals, and celebrate successes.

<u>Wisdom (noun):</u> Is the ability to think and act using knowledge, experience, understanding, common sense and insight.

Reflection:

Professionally, who has provided you with wisdom and support? Describe their words, demeanor, and message.

_____

_____

_____

_____

_____

_____

_____

_____

_____

Words of Inspiration:

"Let the message of Christ dwell among you richly as you teach and admonish one another with all wisdom through psalms, hymns, and songs from the Spirit, singing to God with gratitude in your hearts."

Colossians 3:16

Knowing yourself is the beginning of all wisdom.

— Aristotle

My thoughts:

Over the years, I gained great wisdom from veteran administrators who ultimately became my mentors. These individuals reminded me to always keep the students first. When faced with tough decisions, I would always ask myself, "What is best for kids?"

Strength (noun): The quality or state of being physically strong.

Strengths are tasks or actions you can do well. These include knowledge, proficiencies, skills, and talents. People use their traits and abilities to complete work, relate with others, and achieve goals.

Reflection:

As a school leader, how do you find strength to continue learning and growing in your career?

_____

_____

_____

_____

_____

_____

_____

_____

Words of Inspiration:

I can do all this through him who gives me strength.

Philippians 4:13

When we long for life without difficulties, remind us that oaks grow strong in contrary winds and diamonds are made under pressure.

— Peter Marshall

My thoughts:

Talk about strength...I love to share the story of how I started my dissertation courses on 10/10/11-in the hospital giving birth to twins. It was a scheduled C-section so the good thing is I knew in advance and I was able to make contact with my chair and professor prior to the start of the course.

Honesty (noun): Is a facet of moral character that connotes positive and virtuous attributes such as integrity, truthfulness, straightforwardness, including straightforwardness of conduct, along with the absence of lying, cheating, or theft.

Reflection:

Think of a time when you had to be brutally honest? Why did you choose honesty instead of stretching the truth and feeling more comfortable?

_____

_____

_____

_____

_____

_____

_____

Words of Inspiration:

"If you know his will and approve of what is superior because you are instructed by the law; if you are convinced that you are a guide for the blind, a light for those who are in the dark, an instructor of the foolish, a teacher of little children, because you have in the law the embodiment of knowledge and truth— you, then, who teach others, do you not teach yourself? You who preach against stealing, do you steal? You who say that people should not commit adultery, do you commit adultery? You who abhor idols, do you rob temples? You who boast in the law, do you dishonor God by breaking the law?"

Romans 2:18-23

If you do not tell the truth about yourself you cannot tell it about other people.

— Virginia Woolf

My thoughts:

It's tough being honest sometimes especially with struggling teachers. I always found that the crucial conversations of "Your teaching strategies are not working" or "You are an ineffective teacher" were best communicated with an honest approach. By doing this, I opened the conversation to more constructive feedback and opportunities for growth. I always disliked the approach of other administrators of "being nice" or providing a vague response just to avoid the conversation. This practice is dishonest and negative. Furthermore, it opens the door for the recipient to find out the truth later thus causing long term hard feelings and resentment.

Integrity (noun): Do what's right, legally and morally. Integrity is a quality you develop by adhering to moral principles. It requires that you do and say nothing that deceives others.

Reflection:

How do you promote integrity in your students and leadership team?

_____

_____

_____

_____

_____

_____

_____

_____

Words of Inspiration:

"In everything, set them an example by doing what is good. In your teaching, show integrity, seriousness and soundness of speech that cannot be condemned, so that those who oppose you may be ashamed because they have nothing bad to say about us."

Titus 2:7-8

Listen with curiosity. Speak with honesty. Act with integrity. The greatest problem with communication is we don't listen to understand. We listen to reply. When we listen with curiosity, we don't listen with the intent to reply. We listen for what's behind the words.

— Roy T. Bennett

My thoughts:

Integrity is a value that we teach our students. In my years as an administrator, we had Principal's Advisory Councils, Peer Mentors as well as other student leadership groups. I saw these groups as opportunities to build leadership and not just act as another school activity for students to put on their college applications. I wanted it to be a meaningful opportunity to grow and learn about themselves. Therefore, I would use motivational teen stories and books that talked about leading others and focusing on key values such as integrity, honesty, and leadership. As I reflect on this strategy, I am glad I did it. I hope many of the students that I worked with can look back and see that it was a valuable experience for them.

Energy (noun): The strength and vitality required for sustained physical or mental activity.

Reflection:

What currently has your energy or focus?

___

Words of Inspiration:

"I pray that out of his glorious riches he may strengthen you with power through his Spirit in your inner being, so that Christ may dwell in your hearts through faith. And I pray that you, being rooted and established in love, may have power, together with all the Lord's holy people, to grasp how wide and long and high and deep is the love of Christ, and to know this love that surpasses knowledge—that you may be filled to the measure of all the fullness of God."

Ephesians 3:16-19

Energy and persistence conquer all things.

— Benjamin Franklin

My thoughts:

As an administrator, my energy and focus would shift based on what was going on. For example, during the summer my energy was on getting the year started and making sure that we hired quality staff members to join our team. During winter and spring, state testing and getting Seniors to graduate absorbed a lot of my time and energy. So what does placing your energy on certain areas say about you as an administrator? Well, the items that I named showed that I cared about quality staff for students and students performing well academically and graduating. I think sometimes, our energy shifts to the stressors of mandates and district level initiatives that we forget about the most important people and that is our students. While other things may need to take our energy for a time, my word of advice is "Don't let it sit too long and steal your joy."

Equity (noun): The quality of being fair and impartial.

Reflection:

Have you created any policies or rules that promote equity in your school or district? If so, explain. If not, think of a policy or rule that you would like to create to promote equity in your school or district.

_____

_____

_____

_____

_____

_____

_____

_____

_____

_____

Words of Inspiration:

"Not many of you should become teachers, my fellow believers, because you know that we who teach will be judged more strictly. We all stumble in many ways. Anyone who is never at fault in what they say is perfect, able to keep their whole body in check."

James 3:1-2

Whatever is my right as a man is also the right of another.

— Thomas Paine

My thoughts:

I am reminded of the differences between equity and equality which I use to teach to my graduate students in my "Community of Learners" class. Equity is being fair while equality is making sure that things are equal. This is especially important with staff and students. I can ensure equity without neglecting equality. In other words, I can be fair and make sure that each person has what they need to be successful.

Because of the LORD's great love we are not consumed, for his compassions never fail. They are new every morning; great is your faithfulness.
Lamentations 3:22-23

"The student is not above the teacher, but everyone who is fully trained will be like their teacher."
– Luke 6:40

www.ingramcontent.com/pod-product-compliance
Lightning Source LLC
LaVergne TN
LVHW051505070426
835507LV00022B/2940